Thank you so much for choosing our activity book for your little ones! We truly hope that our book brings joy and learning to your family.

We would be honored if you could spare a moment to leave a review of our book. Your feedback is invaluable to us and helps us improve and reach more families in need of educational and entertaining resources.

Thank you again for choosing our activity book, and we can't wait to hear what you and your kids think!

D1364770

This Book Belongs To

_ _

_ _

Copyright © 2023. All rights reserved.
This book or any portion thereof may not be reproduced or used in any manner whatsoever without express written permission of the publisher

Welcome aboard the
"Airplane Activity Book for Kids Ages 8-12"!

Are you ready for an epic airplane journey filled with fun activities and puzzles? This activity book is packed with over 80 exciting games and challenges that will keep you entertained for hours. From word search and coloring to designing your own airplane and finding your way through mazes, this book is the perfect way to have fun during your flight.

So buckle up, stow your carry-on luggage, and let's embark on a high-flying adventure that you'll never forget!

Let's get started!

The Journey Begins

Where are you going?

- -

When are you traveling?

- -

How long will you be traveling for?

- -

Who will you be traveling with?

- -

Draw what you're most excited to see

Have you been to this destination before?

- -

What are you most excited to see or do on your trip?

- -

- -

Do you have any special plans or events scheduled during your trip?

- -

- -

The weather will be:

My Personal Passport

Design your own passport and go on a world adventure! Personalize it with your own info and dream places to visit. Where will your passport take you? Let's find out together!

Personal Information

Name: _

Date of birth: _ _ _ _ _ _ _ _ _ _ _ _ _ _ _ _ _ _

Place of birth: _ _ _ _ _ _ _ _ _ _ _ _ _ _ _ _ _

nationality: _ _ _ _ _ _ _ _ _ _ _ _ _ _ _ _ _ _

Date of Issue: _ _ _ _ _ _ _ _ _ _ _ _ _ _ _ _

Signature

Places I Visited

Dream Places To Visit

Airport Adventure Maze

Ready for an exciting challenge? Help a family catch their plane in the 'Airport Adventure' maze! Let's go!"

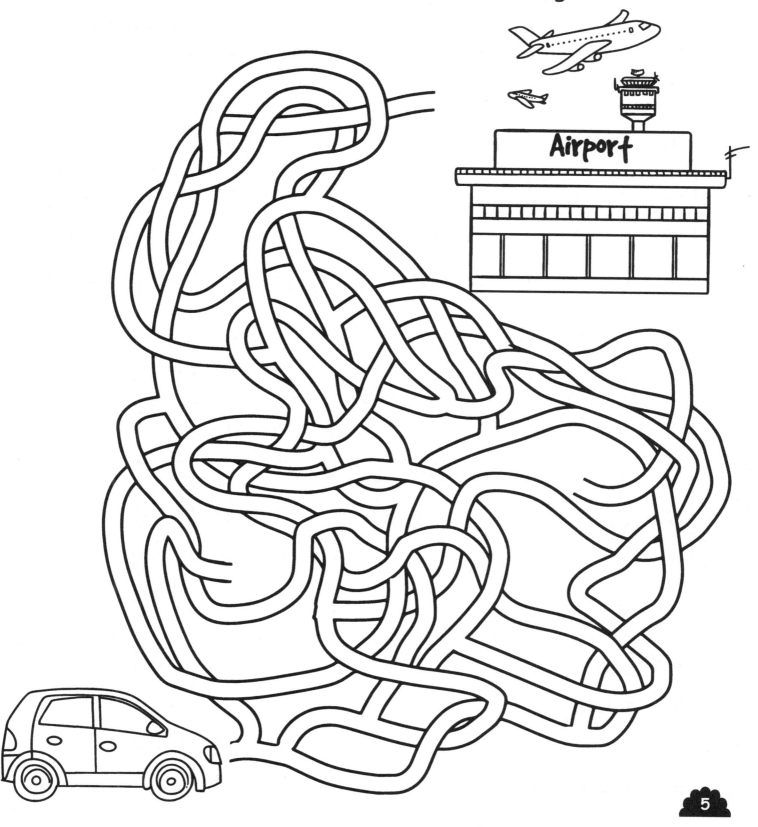

Word Search #1

Get your eyes and brains ready, because it's time to search for hidden words! Can you find them all?

```
F V V E E F R S N W V D L
A D V E N T U R E L A A Q
F U Z K A S V F I M C L A
S X L L I C L S U P A T Q
H U A I R P O R T S T I I
Z V Q X P S E C U R I T Y
C O Q W L G A O K L O U T
H V K P A N R A A P N D I
V A W G N I R V M G I E C
T F G G E V I B O U D T K
W A W U S D V L O U N G E
B T U S R P A S S P O R T
R Q M G Q Q L B W F U O V
```

Adventure	Baggage	Altitude
Vacation	Ticket	Cockpit
Airports	Arrival	Passport
Security	Airplanes	Lounge

Drawing Activity

Put your artistic talents to use by replicating the image with your own drawing skills

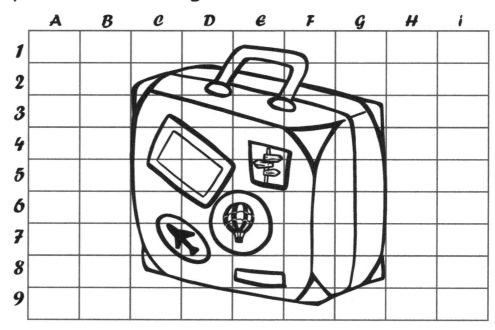

Flying Fun Facts

The Wright brothers are credited with inventing and building the world's first successful airplane in 1903.

Did You Know?

In 1914, the first commercial flight with passengers took off! The plane, called an airboat and flown by a pilot named Tony Jannus, left from St. Petersburg in Florida and landed in Tampa.

The world's busiest airport is Hartsfield-Jackson Atlanta International Airport in Georgia, USA.

Did You Know?

Planes need special wing shapes called aerofoils or airfoils to generate enough lift to balance their weight for flying. Without these special wings, planes would not be able to take off and fly!

Can you solve the secret code and uncover the hidden answer

a	b	c	d	e	f	h	i	l	m	n
1	2	3	4	5	6	7	8	9	10	11

o	p	r	s	t	u	v
12	13	14	15	16	17	18

What happens when you wear a watch on a plane?

16	8	10	5		6	9	8	5	15

Why did the computer go to the doctor?

2	5	3	1	17	15	5		8	16		7	1	4

1		18	8	14	17	15

What's red and smells like blue paint?

14	5	4		13	1	8	11	16

Airplane Acrostic Poem #1

An acrostic poem is a type of poem where the first letter of each line spells out a word or phrase. All lines should relate to or Describe the poem.
Write an acrostic poem for the word below

Pilot

P _____

i _____

L _____

O _____

T _____

Lost and Found

Embark on an exciting adventure with Sarah as she searches for her lost luggage! Follow the numbered path from 1 to 20 to help her find her bags

1	4	5	6	7
1	2	3	8	5
1	2	4	3	8	9	10
9	7	5	6	7	10	3
3	10	1	8	5	11	7
4	2	12	14	13	12	2
12	13	16	15	11	16	19
15	9	17	4	5		
16	10	18	19	20		

Anagram Challenge #1

Put your brain to the test and unscramble the names of essential items for your travels!

Ckoss

- -

Hototrbosh

- -

Sposarpt

- -

Sungaslse

- -

Skobo

- -

Narwdereu

- -

Crossword Game #1

Across

2. This is the type of transportation that travels on tracks and is often used for long-distance travel

4. This document allows you to travel internationally

6. This is the place where you stay overnight when you are away from home

8. This is the document you need to board a plane

10. This is the mode of transportation used to travel long distances through the air

Down

1. This is where airplanes take off and land

3. This is the location where you go to get o a plane

5. This is the type of food that is served o an airplane

7. This is the item used to secure your belongings when traveling

9. This is the person who flies the airplane

Word Search #2

Get your eyes and brains ready, because it's time to search for hidden words! Can you find them all?

```
I G Y F L I G H T F X C W
D E S T I N A T I O N Y U
F T E U I U E E C L U T W
V A A P F G A R V U C V Y
O W T V V W Z M R G U J X
I A B O A R D I N G S D F
E Y E B L C N N G A T L J
D H L P Z E X A S G O M X
M K T A V P L L M E M Q I
D K Y U O T O U R I S M B
D Y O G E L L L B X Q R L
T S E J O U R N E Y W C T
G V B W I X J O J H W M X
```

Destination   **Souvenir**   **Boarding**

Getaway   **Terminal**   **Jet lag**

Tourism   **Customs**   **Luggage**

Journey   **Flight**   **Seatbelt**

Neck Pillow Counting Activity

Let's count together! Keep track of the nock pillows and fill in the blanks

(pillow)(pillow)(pillow) + (pillow)(pillow) = ☐

(pillow) + = 2

(pillow)(pillow) + (pillow)(pillow)(pillow)(pillow)(pillow) = ☐

(pillow)(pillow)(pillow)(pillow) + = 9

(pillow) + (pillow)(pillow)(pillow) = ☐

(pillow)(pillow)(pillow) + (pillow)(pillow)(pillow) = ☐

(pillow)(pillow)(pillow)(pillow) + = 8

(pillow) + (pillow)(pillow) = ☐

Safe Landing Maze

Join the pilot in safely bringing the plane to land. Can you navigate the maze to help the plane touch down smoothly?

Ticket Design

Get Your Tickets Here! Create a Cool and Professional Template for Your Round-Trip Adventure

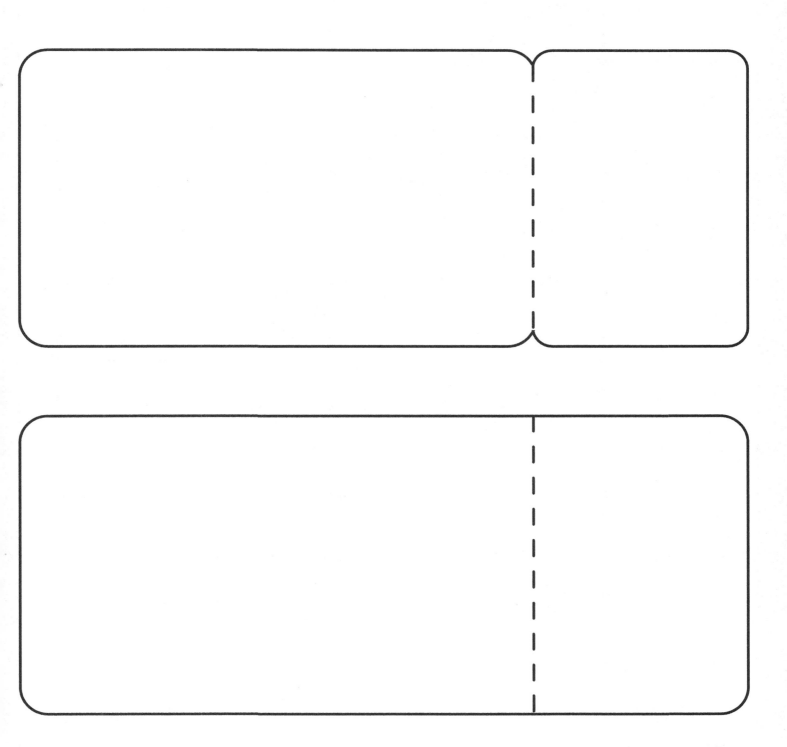

Drawing Activity

Put your artistic talents to use by replicating the image with your own drawing skills

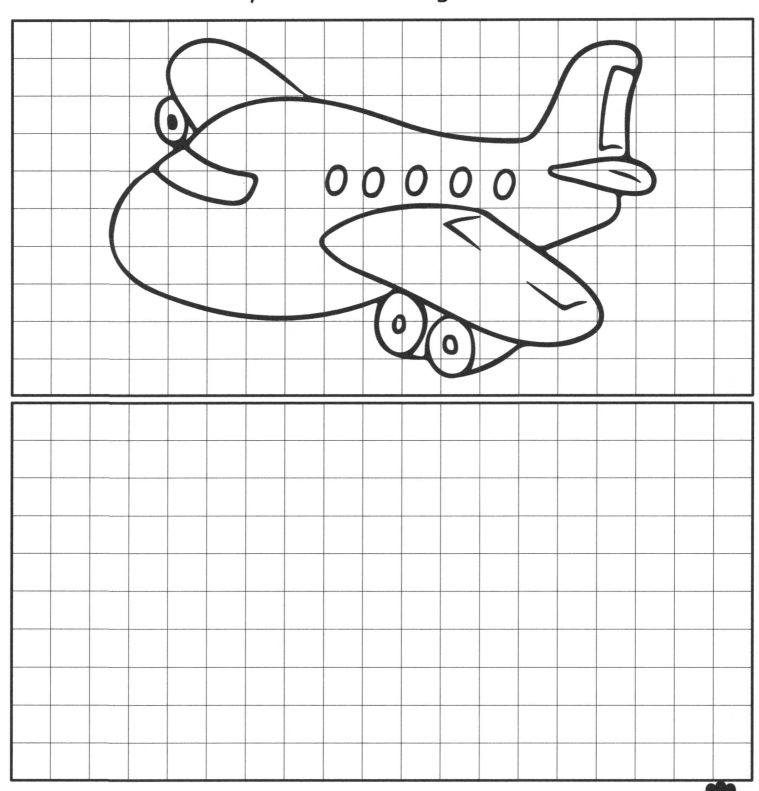

Flying Fun Facts

The biggest plane for carrying people is called the Airbus A380. It's so huge that it can take up to 853 passengers on board

Did You Know?

The longest airplane ride you can take is from Singapore to New York, USA? It's a super long trip that covers a distance of 16,700 kilometers! That's like flying across the whole United States more than four times!

Airplanes need a lot of fuel to take off, but once they're up in the air, they're like super smart and use less fuel than cars or trucks!

Did You Know?

Airplanes need really strong tires to carry them and move really fast. These tires are made special so they can handle the heavy weight of the plane and the super-fast speeds it goes

Connect The Dots #1

Let's start at the number 1 and connect it to the next number in order. Keep going until you finish the drawing

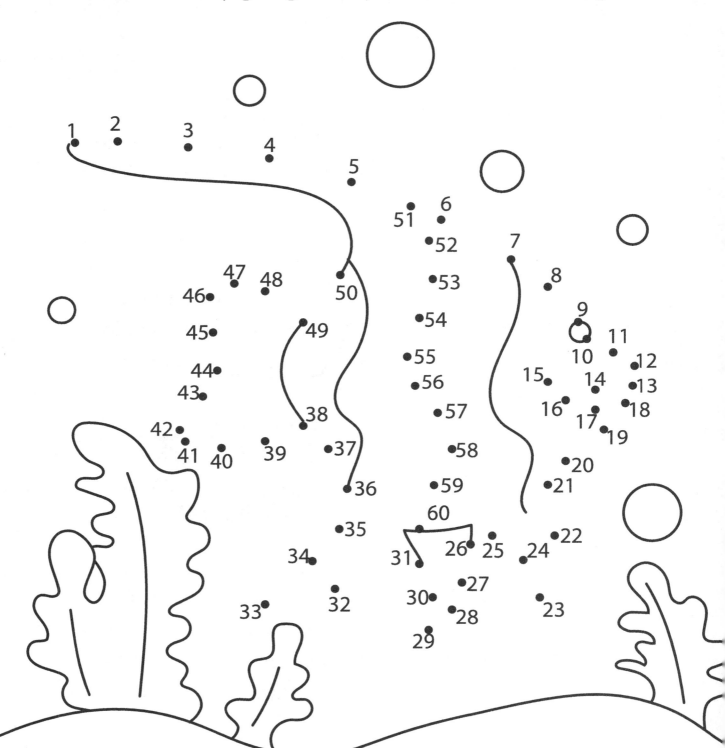

Joke Decoding Adventure #2

Can you solve the secret code and uncover the hidden answer

a	b	c	d	e	f	h	i	l	m	n
1	2	3	4	5	6	7	8	9	10	11

o	p	r	s	t	u	v
12	13	14	15	16	17	18

What has a nose and flies but can't smell?

			1	8	14	13	9	1	11	5
1	11									

Why did the airplane get sent to his room?

			1	9	16	8	16	17	4	5
2	1	4								

What do you call an illegally parked frog?

16	12	1	4

What gives you the power to walk through a wall?

1	4	12	12	14

Airplane Scramble Game #1

Look at the letters around the picture.
Try to rearrange them to fill in the blanks

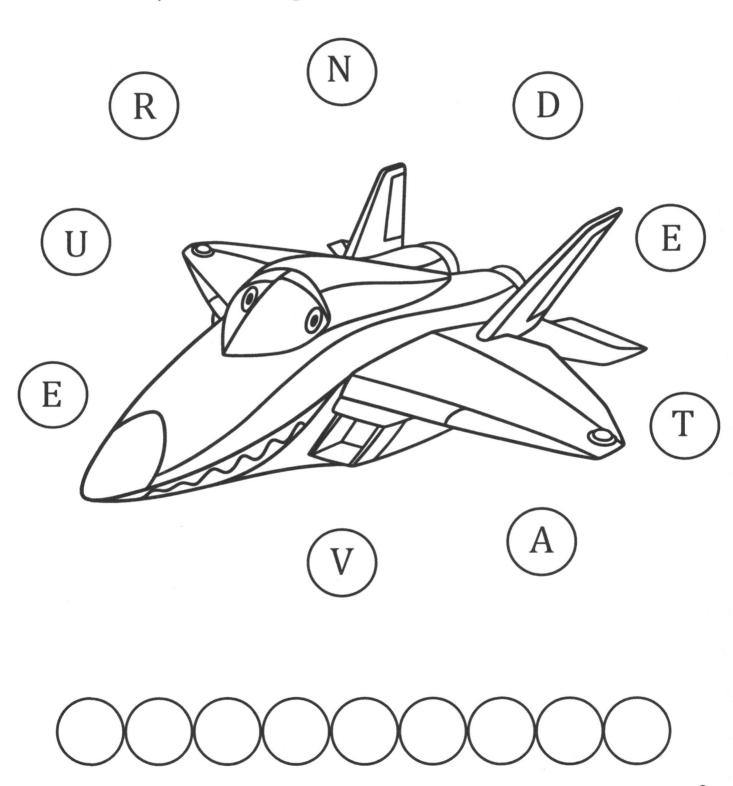

Airplane Doodles

Let your creativity soar! Grab a pencil and paper to doodle fun and colorful drawings inspired by airplanes or anything that sparks your imagination

Odd and Even Numbers

Let's find the tickets with even numbers! Can you circle them?

10	15	36
9	20	3
41	99	81
68	22	12
75	37	13
8	10	49
16	2	35
1	28	41

Airplane Acrostic Poem #2

An acrostic poem is a type of poem where the first letter of each line spells out a word or phrase. All lines should relate to or Describe the poem.
Write an acrostic poem for the word below

Plane

P _

L _

A _

N _

E _

Airplane Math

Time to show off your math skills! Help the little boy find his way to the plane by coloring only the circles that have even numbers inside!

54 x 5 =

37 x 3 =

85 x 7 =

53 x 9 =

26 x 6 =

86 x 9 =

48 x 2 =

27 x 7 =

87 x 3 =

79 x 5 =

37 x 8 =

88 x 7 =

75 x 6 =

64 x 4 =

98 x 3 =

96 x 5 =

47 x 9 =

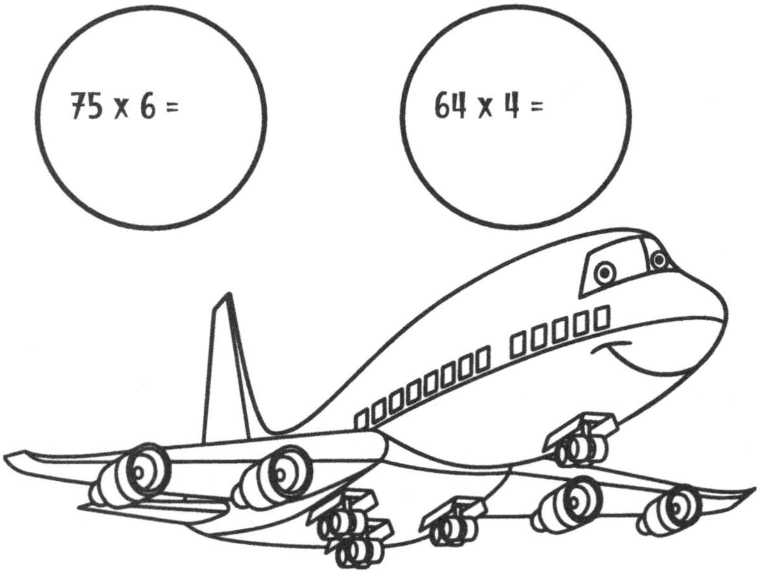

Find Your Seat Maze

Oh no! The airplane is full and it's hard to find your seat! Help by following the path through the maze of people and find your assigned seat!

Bird's Eye View!

Looking out the window, what can you see? Draw the view from your seat on the plane!

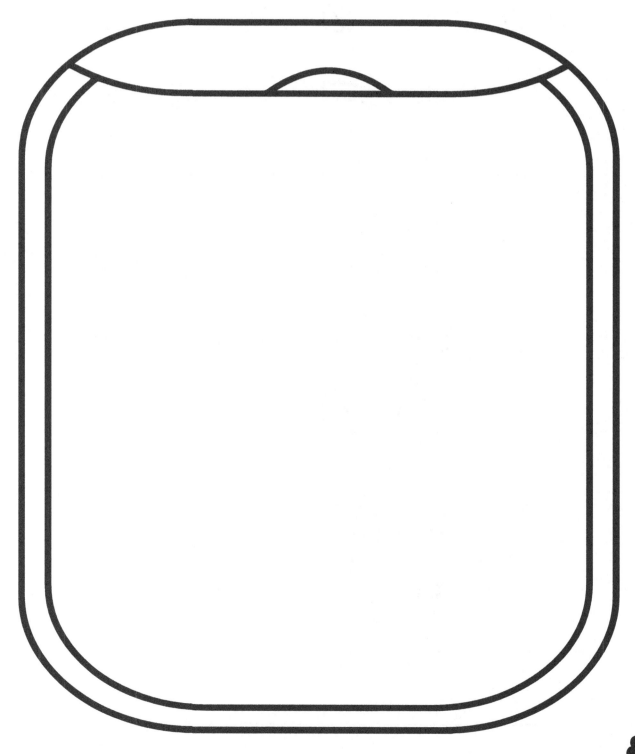

Drawing Activity

Mirror the image! Finish the right side of the picture by copying the lines from the left side

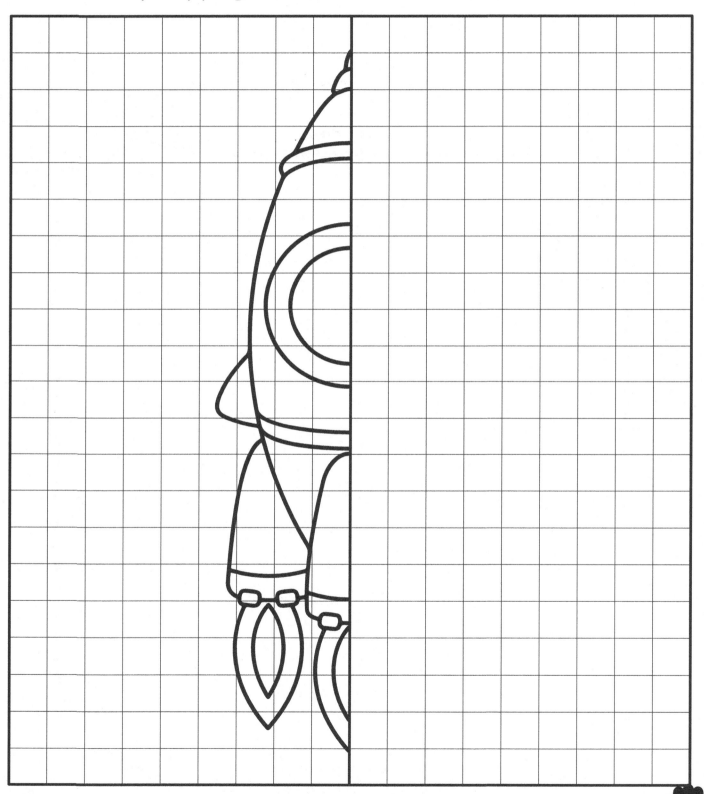

Anagram Challenge #2

Put your brain to the test and unscramble the names of essential items for your travels!

Mphsoao

- -

Tkcite

- -

Kscasn

- -

Strihs

- -

Aretw Botlet

- -

Tkeajcs

- -

Guess The Name #1

Get ready for some brain-teasing fun! Can you guess the name of the pilot and the airplane? Put on your thinking cap and give it a try!

	1	2	3	4	5	6
A	K	C	U	I	W	F
B	G	X	N	E	Q	L
C	A	M	D	O	S	V
D	B	E	Z	Y	T	A
E	N	L	P	I	F	C
F	N	U	X	K	A	B

C3	F5	E1	A4	D2	B6

E5	A6	B2	C5	A3	D4

	1	2	3	4	5	6
A	X	T	N	A	M	O
B	R	E	J	C	Q	P
C	I	D	K	V	I	U
D	L	E	O	G	Z	S
E	Y	X	H	R	B	D
F	C	V	T	W	A	R

Airplane Journaling!

Time to get creative! Draw or write about your travel adventure so far and what you imagine your destination will be like. Will there be palm trees? Snowy mountains? Your imagination is the limit!

Spot The Difference! #1

Can you spot the 5 things that are different in these pictures?

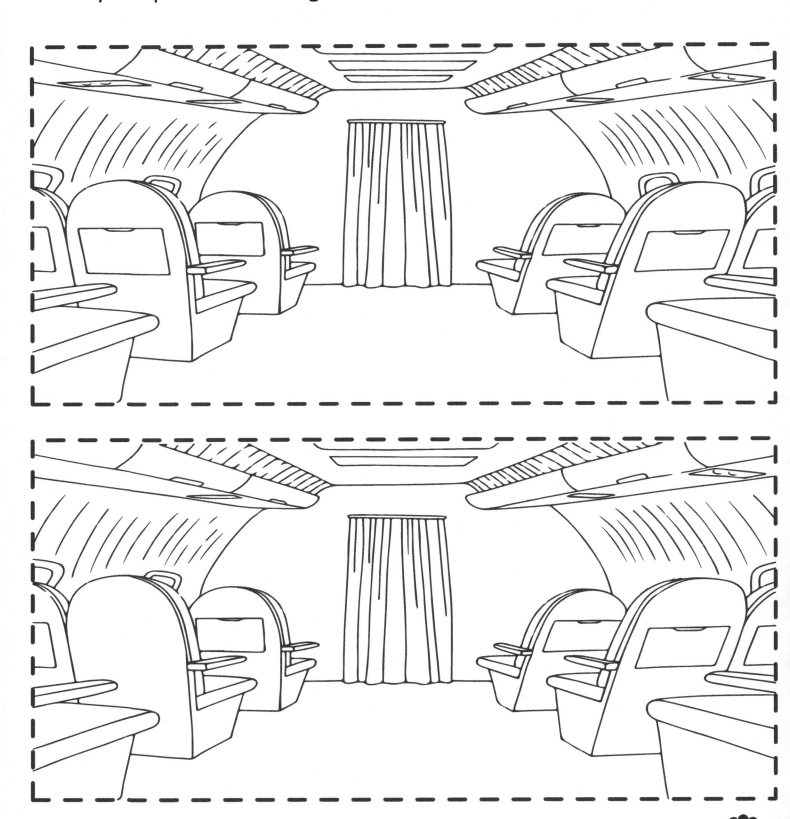

Crossword Game #2

Down

1. This is the person who assists you on the airplane

2. This is where airplanes take off and land

3. This is the item you use to communicate with others when you are away from home

4. This is the part of the airplane that helps it fly

5. This is a small, lightweight device used for taking pictures and capturing memories

8. What do you call the device that measures how heavy luggage is?

9. What do you call the plastic tray that you put your belongings in when you go through security?

Across

6. This is the part of the airport where you pick up your luggage

7. This is the location where you wait to board your airplane

9. What do you call the special section of airplane where first-class passengers sit?

Word Search #3

Get your eyes and brains ready, because it's time to search for hidden words! Can you find them all?

```
N W F Y X L H Z Y P H L C
B W C A R R Y O N I F F W
M T L H E T U I N L F P W
X Q F E E J U K P O U A D
N C P A R C L T E T T S R
C J M D R A K K V Q P S R
H H Q P J D A I S N L E S
C A U H A T T E N D A N T
L A Y O V E R R C Q N G D
W V H N X J D H A U E E H
J E T E N G I N E V R R K
C S Y S A E W V P R E M D
Z T U R B U L E N C E L L
```

Take off	**Carry-on**	**Layover**
Turbulence	**Check-in**	**Travel**
Jet engine	**attendant**	**Pilot**
Headphones	**Passenger**	**Plane**

Airplane Scramble Game #2

Look at the letters around the picture.
Try to rearrange them to fill in the blanks

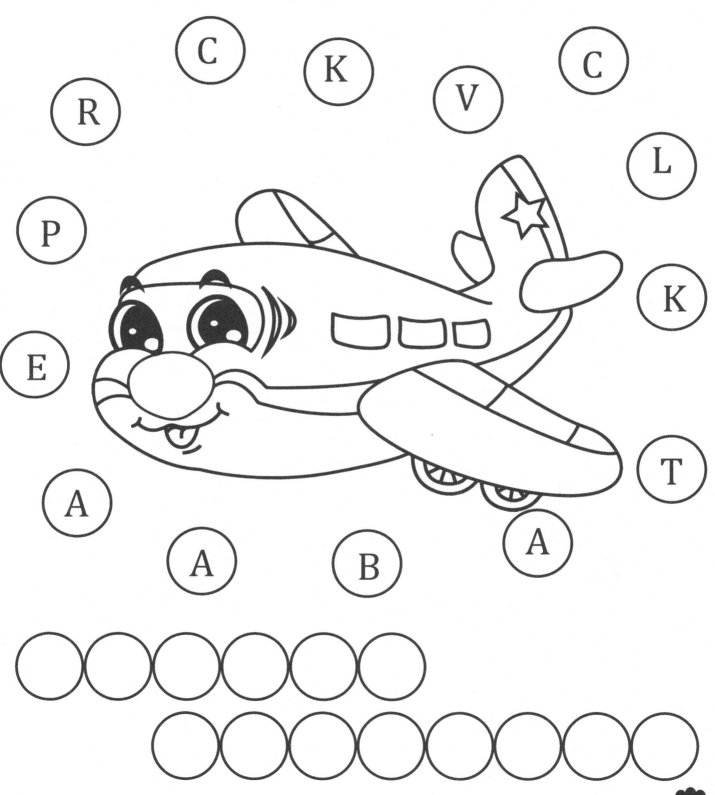

Let's start at the number 1 and connect it to the next number in order. Keep going until you finish the drawing

Flying Fun Facts

The cockpit is the area at the front of the plane where the pilots sit and control the plane.

Did You Know?

The shortest passenger flight in the world is only one minute long? It's called the Loganair Westray to Papa Westray route! Some people have even done it in just 53 seconds - that's super fast!

The fastest plane is called the Boeing 747-8. It has four engines - two on its wings and two on its tail - that help it go really fast! It can go as fast as 658 miles per hour

Did You Know?

Henry Ford wanted to make a hotel for people who visited the airport. He asked a famous architect named Albert Kahn to make a special hotel called the Dearborn Inn. It was the first hotel in the world that was made for an airport.

Emoji Math

Put your math skills to the test and find the value of each?

🐵 + 💛 = 😦 + 1

😄 + 😄 = 🐵

5 = 😄 + 😦

😦 - 3 = 1

🐵 = ☐   💛 = ☐   😦 = ☐

😄 = ☐

Joke Decoding Adventure #3

Can you solve the secret code and uncover the hidden answer

a	b	c	d	e	f	h	i	l	m	n
1	2	3	4	5	6	7	8	9	10	11

o	p	r	s	t	u	v
12	13	14	15	16	17	18

What did one plate say to the other?

4	8	11	11	5	14		8	15		12	11		10	5

What did the football player say to the flight attendant?

13	17	16		10	5		8	11		3	12	1	3	7

What do you call a dinosaur with a extensive vocabulary?

1		16	7	5	15	1	17	14	17	15

43

Airplane Sudoku #1

Solve the following puzzles using the letters T, R,I,P. Each 2x2 Square can have exactly one of each letter. each raw and column can have exactly one of each letter.
This way the whole puzzle is full of lots of love

T			P
R		I	

		P	
	T		
			R
I			

Create Your Own Neck Pillow

Get ready for a comfy journey! Use your imagination to design your very own neck pillow that's perfect for your travel style

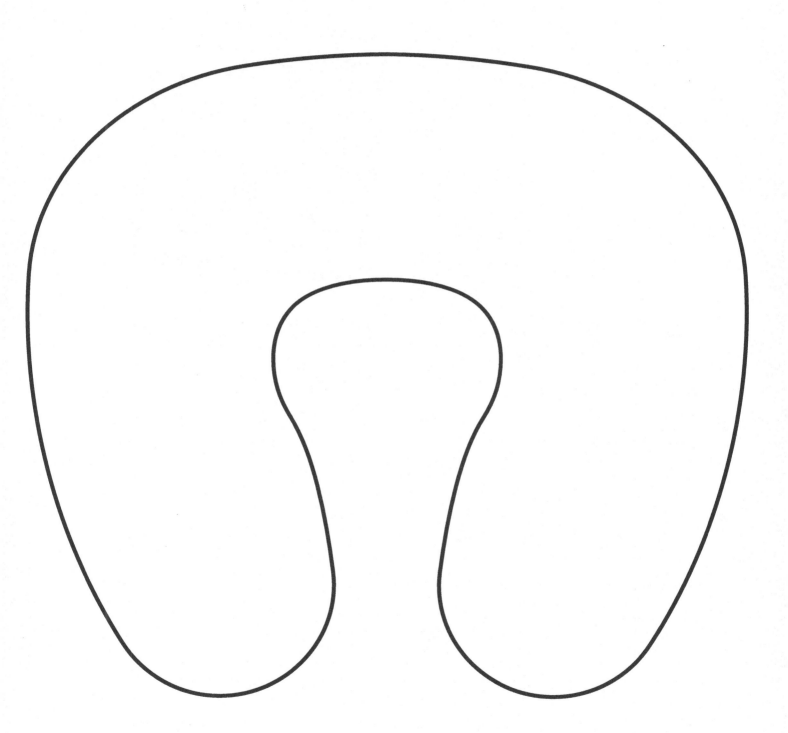

Drawing Activity

Put your artistic talents to use by replicating the image with your own drawing skills

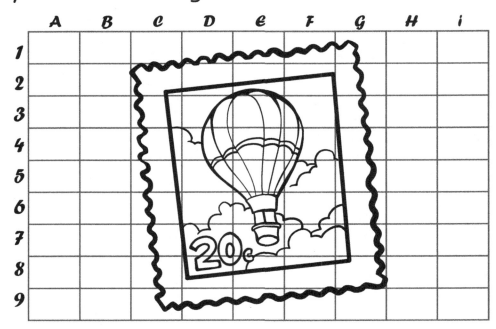

A Journey Through The Airport

Join Jack on an exciting adventure as he searches for his plane in the busy airport! Will you help him navigate through the crowds and find his way to the gate?

Guess The Name #2

Get ready for some brain-teasing fun! Can you guess the name of flight attendant and air traffic controller? Put on your thinking cap and give it a try!

	1	2	3	4	5	6
A	K	C	U	I	W	F
B	G	X	N	E	Q	L
C	A	M	D	O	S	V
D	B	E	Z	Y	T	A
E	N	L	P	I	F	J
F	N	U	M	K	A	B

E6	C1	C5	F3	A4	E1	B4

F4	C5	D1	E4	C1	F5	A5

	1	2	3	4	5	6
A	X	T	N	A	M	O
B	R	E	J	C	Q	P
C	I	D	K	V	I	U
D	L	E	O	G	Z	S
E	Y	X	H	L	B	D
F	C	V	T	W	A	R

48

Spot The Difference! #2

Can you spot the 7 things that are different in these pictures?

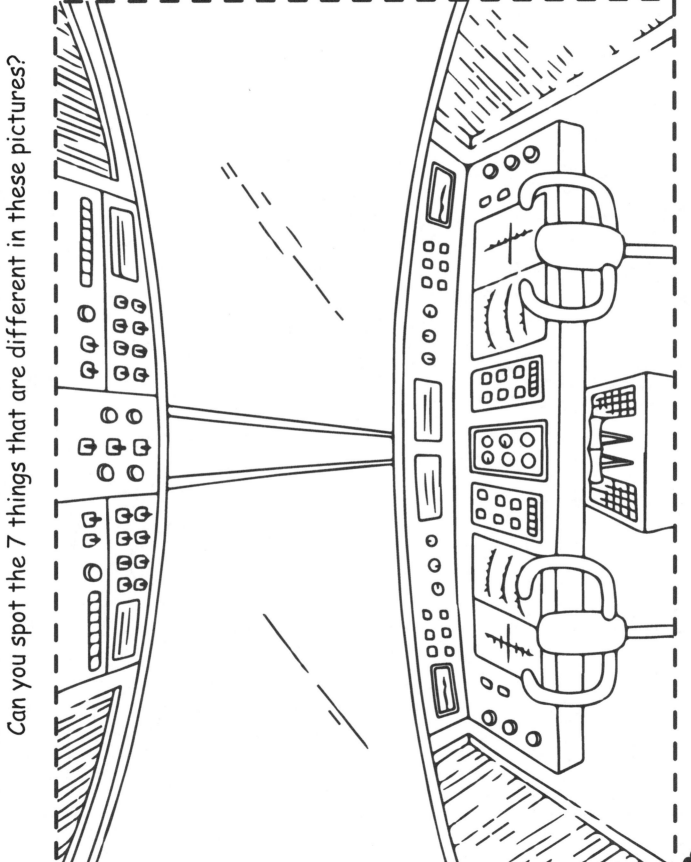

Spot The Difference! #2

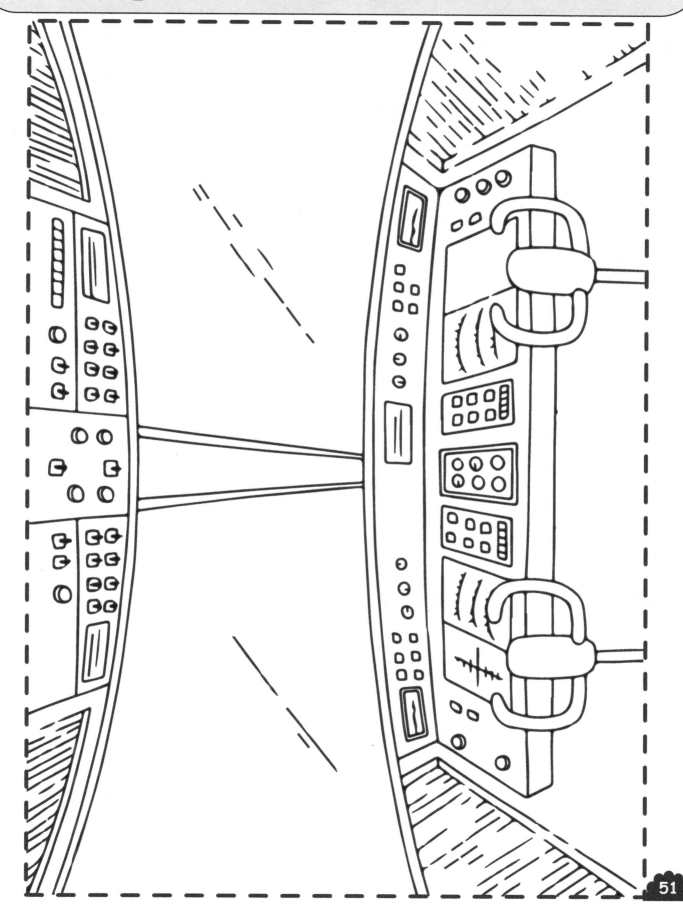

Airplane Acrostic Poem #3

An acrostic poem is a type of poem where the first letter of each line spells out a word or phrase. All lines should relate to or Describe the poem.
Write an acrostic poem for the word below

Travel

T _____

R _____

A _____

V _____

E _____

L _____

Things I Like About Airplanes

Can you name five things you enjoy or appreciate about airplanes?

1) _____

2) _____

3) _____

4) _____

5) _____

Word Search #4

Get your eyes and brains ready, because it's time to search for hidden words! Can you find them all?

```
C I N F L I G H T M E A L
S O H M X I L W K E I I E
X V P A N P R I T Q N R L
L W V I Q R M W X K N C C
N H D N L K D O R Y A R V
Q G H T Y O B D J C V A N
J L O E O K T R F C I F K
S V F N C V M P H L G T Q
Z B O A R D I N G G A T E
A Z L N B R V X T L T P J
X B T C T A V I A T I O N
M C K E C A R G O H O L D
G S I G H T S E E I N G N
```

Navigation   **Aviation**   **Aircraft**

Boarding gate   **Co-pilot**   **Cargo hold**

In-flight meal   **Flap**   **Maintenance**

Sightseeing   **Trip**   **Black box**

Anagram Challenge #3

Put your brain to the test and unscramble the names of essential items for your travels!

Lbatta

- - - - - - - - - - - - - - - - - -

Stsiumiw

- - - - - - - - - - - - - - - - - -

Ahdn Poas

- - - - - - - - - - - - - - - - - -

Keasners

- - - - - - - - - - - - - - - - - -

Hnope

- - - - - - - - - - - - - - - - - -

Plilwos

- - - - - - - - - - - - - - - - - -

Design Your Own Airplane

Let your creativity soar! Become an engineer and designer by building your very own masterpiece airplane!

Flying Fun Facts

Some airports have special areas called observation decks, where people can watch planes take off and land.

The world's largest airplane is called the Antonov An-225 Mriya? It's so huge that it can carry as much as 320 cars or 128 elephants! That's a lot of weight, over 640,000 pounds!

The first flight attendants were all men, and they were hired in the 1920s to help passengers feel more comfortable and safe during flights.

Did You Know?

Airplanes are painted white because it helps to reflect the sunlight and keep the plane from getting too hot. This means less energy is needed to keep the inside of the plane cool and comfortable for everyone

Joke Decoding Adventure #4

Can you solve the secret code and uncover the hidden answer

a	b	c	d	e	f	g	h	k	l	m
1	2	3	4	5	6	7	8	9	10	11

n	o	p	r	s	t	u	v	y
12	13	14	15	16	17	18	19	20

What did the llama say when he got kicked out of the zoo?

1	9	14	1	3	1

11	20

2	1	7	16

How do you stop an astronaut's baby from crying?

20	13	18

15	13	3	9	5	17

What happens to bad plane jokes?

9	8	5	20

12	5	19	5	15

10	1	12	4

58

Airplane Scramble Game #3

Look at the letters around the picture.
Try to rearrange them to fill in the blanks

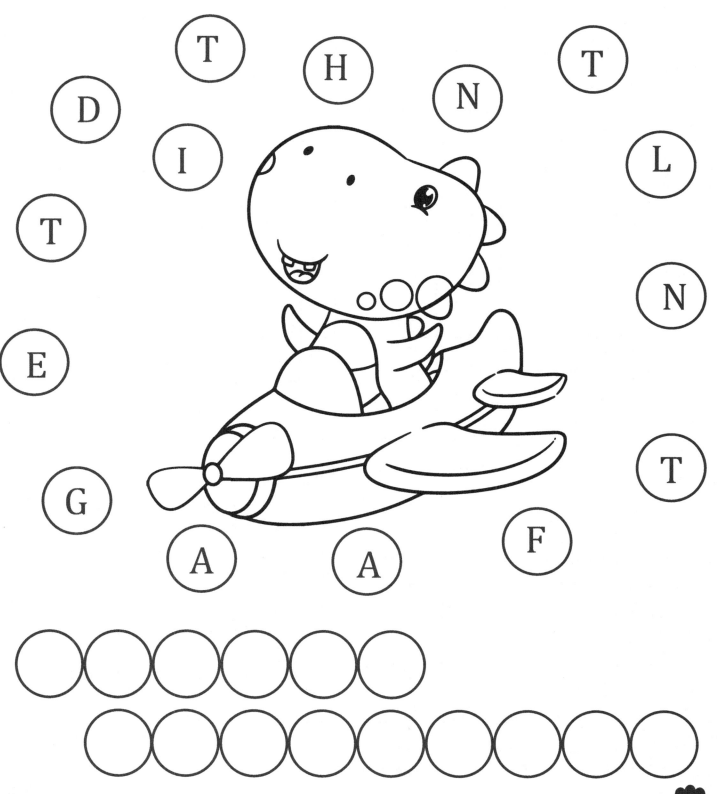

Crossword Game #3

Across

1. Used at takeoff and landing to produce additional force

3. What do you call the large, flat area where airplanes are parked when they are not in use?

6. What do you call the large metal stairs that lead up to the airplane door?

8. The movement of an airplane through the air without the use of engine power.

9. What do you call the long, narrow tubes that connect the airplane to the airport terminal?

10. This is the section of the airplane where the pilot and co-pilot sit

Down

2. The force that propels an airplane forward through the air

4. This is the small bag you can bring with you on the airplane

5. What do you call the people who work on airplanes and make sure they are safe to fly?

7. Force which keeps us on the ground

Create Your Own Suitcase

Let's get creative! Design and decorate your own special suitcase using your imagination!

Airplane Sudoku #2

Solve the following puzzles using the letters T, R, I, P. Each 2x2 Square can have exactly one of each letter. each raw and column can have exactly one of each letter. This way the whole puzzle is full of lots of love

R			
		R	
P			
			I

			T
	T		
			I
	P		

Cloud Hide and Seek

Let's help the cute birds find their cloud hideout! Can you guide them through the busy skies and avoid the airplanes?

Connect The Dots #3

Let's start at the number 1 and connect it to the next number in order. Keep going until you finish the drawing

Design a New Hat for Your Pilot

Uh oh, looks like your pilot lost his hat! Can you help him out by drawing a new one? Make it cool and professional so he can look his best!

Drawing Activity

Mirror the image! Finish the right side of the picture by copying the lines from the left side

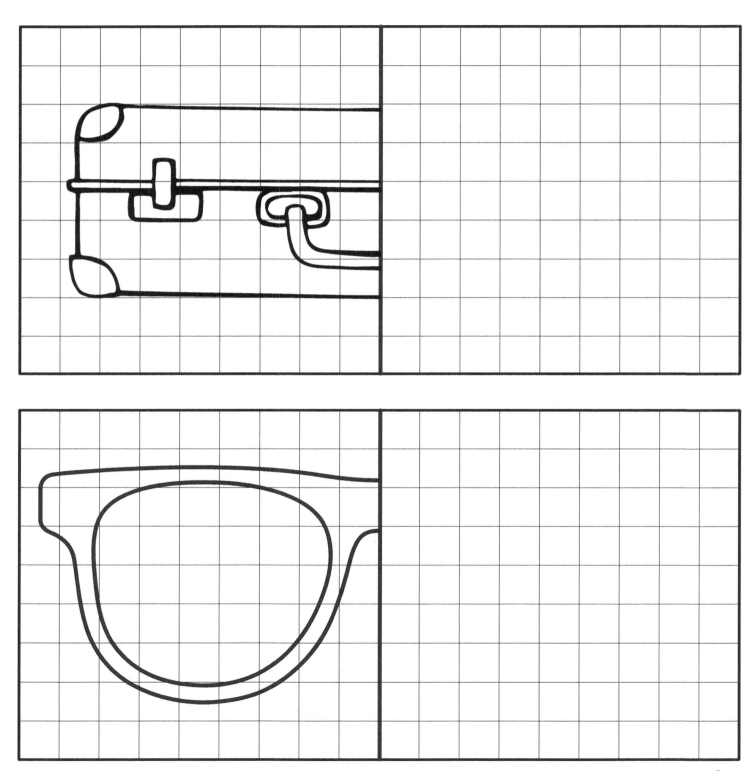

Airplane Window Math

Put your math skills to the test by solving these two-digit addition problems, using regrouping if needed

23
+ 35
_____

47
+ 15
_____

26
+ 30
_____

18
+ 18
_____

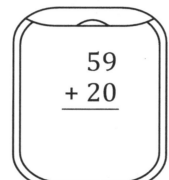

59
+ 20
_____

88
+ 11
_____

37
+ 22
_____

55
+ 44
_____

17
+ 65
_____

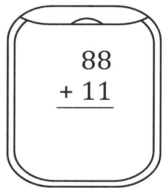

75
+ 15
_____

12
+ 16
_____

31
+ 32
_____

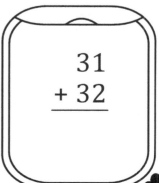

Word Search #5

Get your eyes and brains ready, because it's time to search for hidden words! Can you find them all?

```
A M F L I G H T D E L A Y
K C Q Y G F Q Q F V S I F
U O T P R O P E L L E R O
P N H R O X G O L Y Z T V
Q C R G U H R X A P K R E
K O C D N H E W N Z K A R
K U R W D Y N L D E X F B
E R U U C U C R I W Y F O
N S I K R S O Y N P F I O
D E S C E N T H G A A C K
C E E G W J U D Z A Q D I
G A I R M A R S H A L G N
B N T U K X Q C T S L M G
```

Air traffic	Helipad	Runway
Overbooking	Cruise	Propeller
Ground crew	Descent	Air marshal
Flight delay	Landing	Concourse

Create A Postcard

Use your imagination and art skills to make a postcard of a place you really want to go! Where would you like to go?

Airplane Acrostic Poem #4

An acrostic poem is a type of poem where the first letter of each line spells out a word or phrase. All lines should relate to or Describe the poem.
Write an acrostic poem for the word below

Ticket

T _____

I _____

C _____

k _____

E _____

T _____

Joke Decoding Adventure #5

Can you solve the secret code and uncover the hidden answer

a	b	c	d	e	f	g	h	i	l	m
1	2	3	4	5	6	7	8	9	10	11

n	o	p	r	s	t	u	v	y
12	13	14	15	16	17	18	19	20

What's another name for a flying police officer?

1	8	5	10	9	3	13	14	14	5	15

Everyone knows two wrongs don't make a right, but what do two Wrights make?

1	12	1	9	15	14	10	1	12	5

What sound does a rubber airplane make?

2	12	5	9	12	7

New Hair for Your Seatmate!

Oh no, it looks like the person sitting next to you lost their hair! Can you use your imagination and draw them some new hair? Be creative and use lots of colors to make them look their best when they board the plane!

Anagram Challenge #4

Put your brain to the test and unscramble the names of essential items for your travels!

Tethpoasto

- -

may seek

- -

amacer

- -

suncenser

- -

aimtoendice

- -

rodeotend

- -

Spot The Difference! #3

Can you spot the 10 things that are different in these pictures?

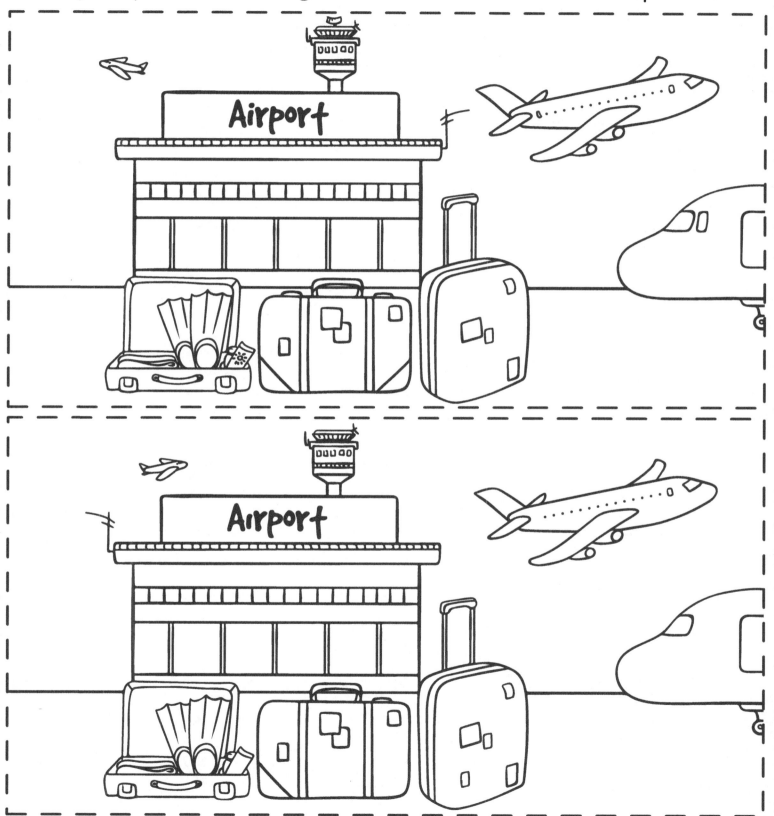

Math Suitcase Challenge

Put your math skills to the test! Use the numbers on the suitcase to solve multiplication problems and fill in the circles to create the perfect equation

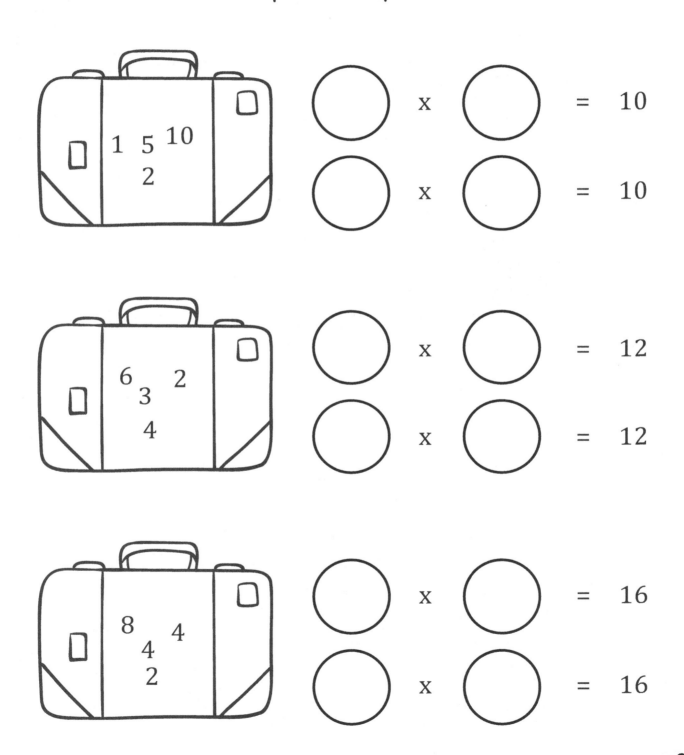

○ x ○ = 10

○ x ○ = 10

○ x ○ = 12

○ x ○ = 12

○ x ○ = 16

○ x ○ = 16

Suitcase 1: 1 5 10 2

Suitcase 2: 6 3 2 4

Suitcase 3: 8 4 4 2

Find the Way

The flight attendant is running late for her flight and needs your help! Can you guide her through the maze to find the plane on time?

Design a Tattoo for Your Pilot

If your pilot had a tattoo, what do you think it would be of?
Draw and color your own tattoo design for your pilot!

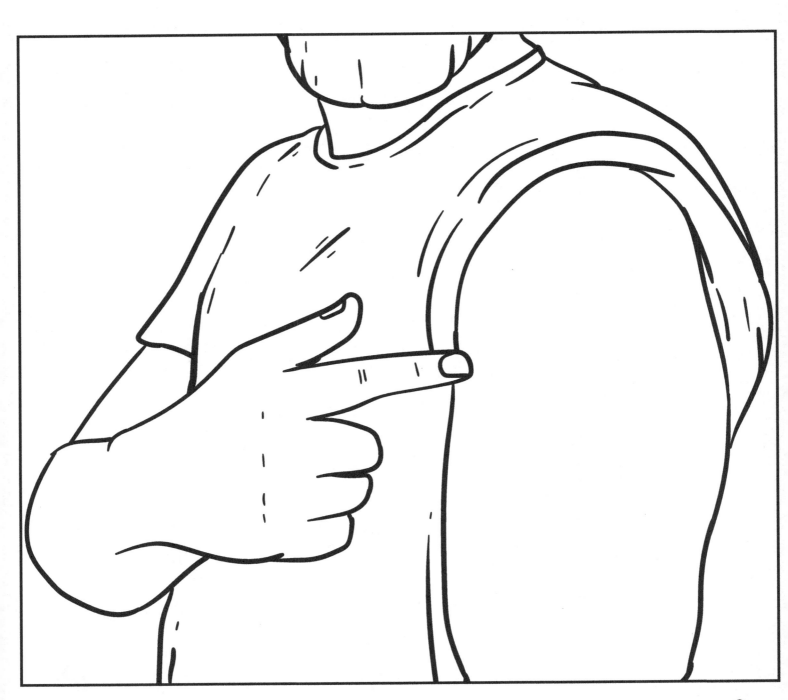

Airplane Scramble Game #4

Look at the letters around the picture.
Try to rearrange them to fill in the blanks

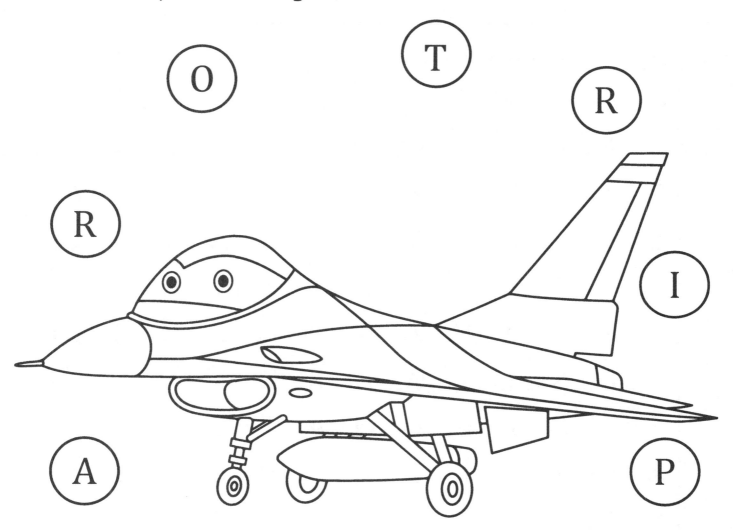

O T R R I A P

Word Search #6

Get your eyes and brains ready, because it's time to search for hidden words! Can you find them all?

```
V  Z  L  I  F  E  V  E  S  T  S  W  I
W  S  Y  A  Q  M  W  C  L  D  T  G  C
A  F  E  C  I  W  W  E  S  E  Y  N  O
Q  I  V  D  I  R  B  V  L  O  I  Q  A
L  R  O  P  E  T  L  T  B  A  V  H  C
I  S  J  R  A  P  Z  I  T  I  C  A  H
S  T  A  E  V  W  A  P  N  Z  Q  Q  C
M  C  S  T  E  W  A  R  D  E  S  S  L
E  L  G  L  G  C  Q  A  T  B  A  Z  A
A  A  I  G  K  Z  A  H  M  U  J  S  S
K  S  T  O  P  O  V  E  R  S  R  W  S
A  S  T  O  V  E  R  B  O  O  K  E  D
H  A  N  D  L  U  G  G  A  G  E  E  S
```

Airline   **Stewardess**   **Stopover**

Captain   **Hand Luggage**   **Overbooked**

First Class   **Seatbelt**   **Asile**

Life Vest   **Departures**   **Coach Class**

Adventures to Remember

Grab your pen, and write down all the amazing moments you experienced on your trip. From the beautiful sights to the fun games you played, capture it all and create a special memory to cherish forever!

Adventures to Remember

Did you know that drawing can be a great way to capture memories? When you draw something, it's like taking a snapshot of it and keeping it forever. So, let's take a moment to remember our airplane trip and all the amazing things we saw along the way. Get your pencils ready, and let's start drawing!

Solutions

Airport Adventure Maze

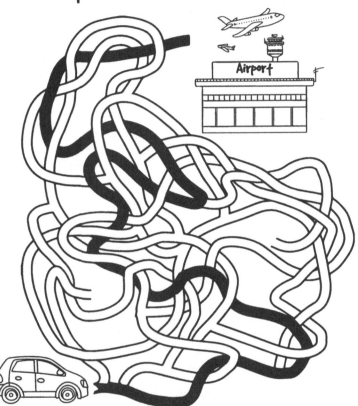

Word Search #1

```
F V V E E F R S N W V D L
A D V E N T U R E L A A Q
F U Z K A S V F I M C L A
S X L L I C L S U P A T Q
H U A I R P O R T S T I I
Z V Q X P S E C U R I T Y
C O Q W L G A O K L O U T
H V K P A N R A A P N D I
V A W G N I R V M G I E C
T F G G E V I B O U D T K
W A W U S D V L O U N G E
B T U S R P A S S P O R T
R Q M G Q Q L B W F U O V
```

Joke Decoding Adventure #1

Q. What happens when you wear a watch on a plane?

A. Time flies

Q. Why did the computer go to the doctor?

A. Because it had a virus

Q. What's red and smells like blue paint?

A. Red paint

Airplane Acrostic Poem #1
(possible answer)

Pilot, steering the plane with skill and care

Into the air and through the clouds we soar

Leading us to new destinations with flair

Onward and upward, higher than ever before

Taking us to places we've never been before.

Lost and Found

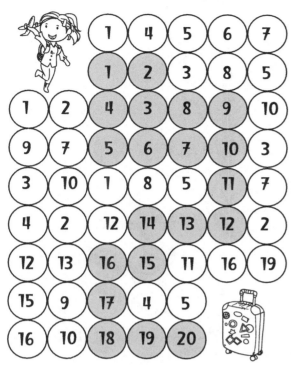

1	4	5	6	7

Grid of numbers:
- 1 2 3 8 5
- 1 2 4 3 8 9 10
- 9 7 5 6 7 10 3
- 3 10 1 8 5 11 7
- 4 2 12 14 13 12 2
- 12 13 16 15 11 16 19
- 15 9 17 4 5
- 16 10 18 19 20

Anagram Challenge #1

Socks
Toothbrush
Passport
Sunglasses
Books
Underwear

Crossword Game #1

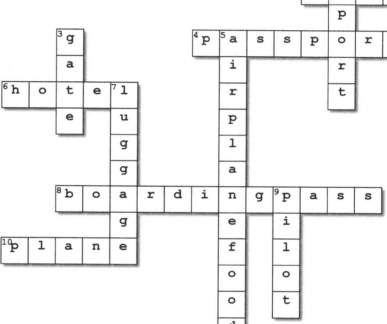

1. a i
2. t r a i n
   p
4. p a s s p o r t (5. a i r p l a n e f o o d)
   o r t
3. g a t e
6. h o t e l (7. l u g g a g e)
8. b o a r d i n g 9. p a s s
   g (e f o o d) (i l o t)
10. p l a n e

Word Search #2

```
I  G  Y  F  L  I  G  H  T  F  X  C  W
D  E  S  T  I  N  A  T  I  O  N  Y  U
F  T  E  U  I  U  E  E  C  L  U  T  W
V  A  A  P  F  G  A  R  V  U  C  V  Y
O  W  T  V  V  W  Z  M  R  G  U  J  X
I  A  B  O  A  R  D  I  N  G  S  D  F
E  Y  E  B  L  C  N  N  G  A  T  L  J
D  H  L  P  Z  E  X  A  S  G  O  M  X
M  K  T  A  V  P  L  M  E  M  Q  I
D  K  Y  U  O  T  O  U  R  I  S  M  B
D  Y  O  G  E  L  L  L  B  X  Q  R  L
T  S  E  J  O  U  R  N  E  Y  W  C  T
G  V  B  W  I  X  J  O  J  H  W  M  X
```

Neck Pillow Counting Activity

🙂🙂🙂 + 🙂🙂 = [5]

🙂 + 🙂 = [2]

🙂🙂 + 🙂🙂🙂🙂🙂 = [7]

🙂🙂🙂🙂 + 🙂🙂🙂🙂🙂 = [9]

🙂 + 🙂🙂🙂 = [4]

🙂🙂🙂 + 🙂🙂🙂 = [6]

🙂🙂🙂🙂 + 🙂🙂🙂🙂 = [8]

🙂 + 🙂🙂 = [3]

Safe Landing Maze

Joke Decoding Adventure #2

Q. What has a nose and flies but can't smell?

A. An airplane

Q. Why did the airplane get sent to his room?

A. Bad altitude

Q. What do you call an illegally parked frog?

A. Toad

Q. What gives you the power to walk through a wall?

A. A door

Airplane Scramble Game #1

Airplane Acrostic Poem #2
(possible answer)

Passing swiftly through the air,

Leaping over mountains with great care,

Above the clouds we soar,

Navigating winds and more,

Elevating us to new heights.

Airplane Math

 54 x 5 =   37 x 3 =   85 x 7 =

 53 x 9 =   26 x 6 =   86 x 9 =   48 x 2 =

 27 x 7 =   87 x 3 =   79 x 5 =   37 x 8 =

 88 x 7 =   75 x 6 =   64 x 4 =   98 x 3 =

 96 x 5 =   47 x 9 =

Find Your Seat Maze

Anagram Challenge #2

Shampoo
Ticket
Snacks
Shirts
Water Bottle
Jackets

Guess the Name #1

pilot = Daniel

plane = Boeing

Crossword Game #2

Across:
6. baggage claim
7. terminal
9. business class

Down:
1. flight
2. runway
3. phone
4. wings
5. came
6. battedae
8. scae

Word Search #3

```
N W F Y X L H Z Y P H L C
B W C A R R Y O N I F F W
M T L H E T U I N L F P W
X Q F E E J U K P O U A D
N C P A R C L T E T T S R
C J M D R A K K V Q P S R
H H Q P J D A I S N L E S
C A U H A T T E N D A N T
L A Y O V E R R C Q N G D
W V H N X J D H A U E E H
J E T E N G I N E V R R K
C S Y S A E W V P R E M D
Z T U R B U L E N C E L L
```

Airplane Scramble Game #2

T R A V E L
B A C K P A C K

Emoji Math

 = 3

 = 4

 = 2

 = 1

Joke Decoding Adventure #3

Q. What did one plate say to the other?

A. Dinner is on me

Q: What did the football player say to the flight attendant?

A: Put me in coach

Q. What do you call a dinosaur with a extensive vocabulary?

A. A thesaurus

Airplane Sudoku #1

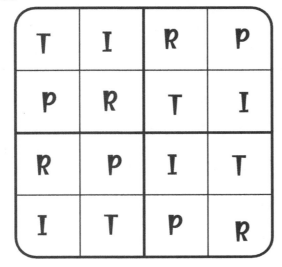

T	I	R	P
P	R	T	I
R	P	I	T
I	T	P	R

R	I	P	T
P	T	R	I
T	P	I	R
I	R	T	P

A Journey Through The Airport

Guess the Name #2

Flight Attendants: Jasmine

Security Guards: William

Airplane Acrostic Poem #3
(possible answer)

Traversing the world with glee,

Roaming far and wide and free,

Adventure waiting at every turn,

Visiting places we yearn,

Experiencing new cultures and ways,

Learning as we explore each new phase.

Word Search #4

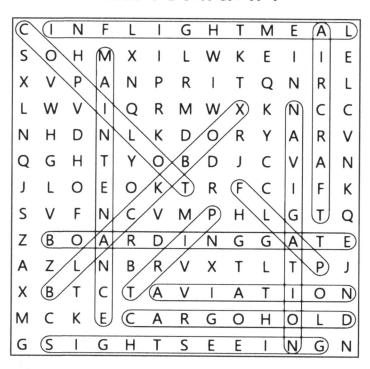

Anagram Challenge #3

Tablet

Swimsuit

Hand Soap

Sneakers

Phone

Pillows

Joke Decoding Adventure #4

Q. What did the llama say when he got kicked out of the zoo?

A. "Alpaca my bags!"

Q. How do you stop an astronaut's baby from crying?

A. You rocket!

Q. What happens to bad plane jokes?

A. They never land

Airplane Scramble Game #3

Airplane Sudoku #2

R	P	I	T
I	T	R	P
P	I	T	R
T	R	P	I

P	I	R	T
R	T	I	P
T	R	P	I
I	P	T	R

Crossword Game #3

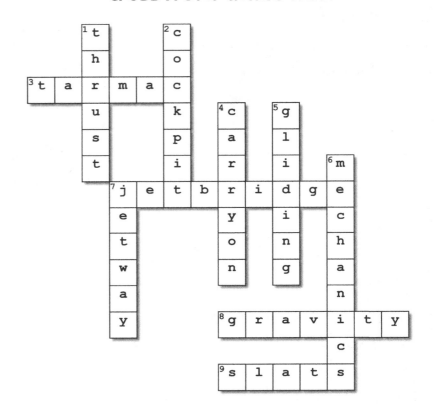

Cloud Hide and Seek

Airplane Window Math

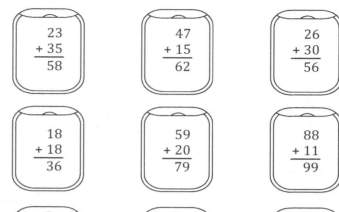
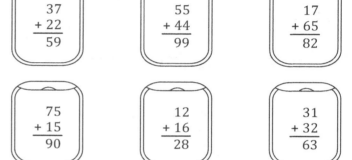

23 + 35 58	47 + 15 62	26 + 30 56
18 + 18 36	59 + 20 79	88 + 11 99
37 + 22 59	55 + 44 99	17 + 65 82
75 + 15 90	12 + 16 28	31 + 32 63

Word Search #5

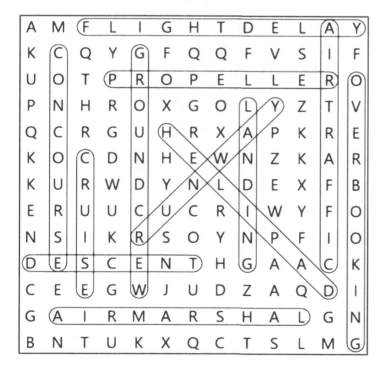

Airplane Acrostic Poem #4
(possible answer)

Take a trip to a new place,

Incredible sights to see,

Curious about the destination,

Kites and clouds as far as we can see,

Expectant for what's in store,

Taking flight with our ticket!

Joke Decoding Adventure #5

Q. What's another name for a flying police officer?

A. A heli-copper

Q. Everyone knows two wrongs don't make a right, but what do two Wrights make?

A. An airplane

Q. What sound does a rubber airplane make?

A. Boeing

Math Suitcase Challenge

$10 \times 1 = 10$

$5 \times 2 = 10$

$6 \times 2 = 12$

$3 \times 4 = 12$

$8 \times 2 = 16$

$4 \times 4 = 16$

Airplane Scramble Game #4

Anagram Challenge #4

Toothpaste

Eye mask

Camera

Sunscreen

Medications

deodorant

Find the Way

Word Search #6

V	Z	L	I	F	E	V	E	S	T	S	W	I
W	S	Y	A	Q	M	W	C	L	D	T	G	C
A	F	E	C	I	W	W	E	S	E	Y	N	O
Q	I	V	D	I	R	B	V	L	O	I	Q	A
L	R	O	P	E	T	L	T	B	A	V	H	C
I	S	J	R	A	P	Z	I	T	I	C	A	H
S	T	A	E	V	W	A	P	N	Z	Q	Q	C
M	C	S	T	E	W	A	R	D	E	S	S	L
E	L	G	L	G	C	Q	A	T	B	A	Z	A
A	A	I	G	K	Z	A	H	M	U	J	S	S
K	S	T	O	P	O	V	E	R	S	R	W	S
A	S	T	O	V	E	R	B	O	O	K	E	D
H	A	N	D	L	U	G	G	A	G	E	F	S

92

Thank you for purchasing our activity book for kids!

We hope your child had fun completing the activities and that the book brought a little bit of fun and creativity into their day.

If you have a moment, we would really appreciate it if you could leave a review on Amazon. Your feedback helps other parents decide if the book is right for their children, and it helps us improve and reach more families in need of educational and entertaining resources. Plus, it's always nice to hear what people think of our work!

Thank you in advance for your help, and we hope you and your child have a great day!

Kindest regards,

Creative Funland

Made in the USA
Middletown, DE
07 June 2023

32248576R00053